# Eye On The Environment
# TRASH

## J.M. Patten, Ed.D.

The Rourke Book Co., Inc.
Vero Beach, Florida 32964

Edited by Pamela J.P. Schroeder and Sandra A. Robinson

PHOTO CREDITS
© J.M. Patten: cover, pages 4, 6, 7, 9, 10, 19, 21, 22; © Mike Naylor: pages 12, 13, 15, 16, 18


**Library of Congress Cataloging-in-Publication Data**

Patten, J.M., 1944-
    Trash / J.M. Patten.
        p.  cm. — (Eye on the environment)
    Includes index.
    ISBN 1-55916-101-9
    1. Refuse and refuse disposal—Juvenile literature.
[1. Refuse and refuse disposal.] I. Title. II. Series.
TD792.P38   1995
363.72'8—dc20                                              94-42670
                                                                CIP
                                                                AC


Printed in the USA

# TABLE OF CONTENTS

Eye on Trash ............................................. 5

What Is Trash? ........................................ 6

Other Kinds of Trash ............................. 8

The Trash Monster ................................ 11

The Trash Trail ....................................... 12

Where Does Trash Go? ....................... 14

Trash and Trouble .............................. 17

Recycling Trash ................................... 18

What Can You Do? .............................. 20

Glossary ................................................ 23

Index ...................................................... 24

# EYE ON TRASH

This book is about problems with trash. You will find out where trash comes from and how it harms the Earth's **environment.**

The Earth's environment is all living and nonliving things in the world. The soil we farm, air we breathe, and water we drink are important parts of the environment. People must work to keep them clean and safe.

Earth is our home—the only known place where people, plants and animals can live. Too much trash damages our home, and hurts us all.

*This discarded, plastic foam container was left along the path for someone else to pick up.*

# WHAT IS TRASH?

Trash is anything people throw away. It's all the things we put in waste baskets, garbage cans and dumpsters.

Trash has lots of names like rubbish, garbage, litter, debris, scraps, refuse and junk.

*Household trash is put in garbage cans that sit at the curb on neighborhood trash day.*

*Large metal appliances that people throw away are called white goods.*

Scientists call trash **solid waste. Liquid waste** is sewage from sinks and toilets. Smoke, exhaust and fumes are **gaseous waste,** or waste in the air.

# OTHER KINDS OF TRASH

When household appliances—like refrigerators, washers and dryers—break, people throw them away. These large, metal throwaways are called *white goods*.

Flashlight batteries, old paint, and hospital bandages and needles are toxic, or poisonous, trash. Toxic trash can make people and animals sick—or even kill them.

In the fall, many children play in the colorful leaves on the ground. Leaves, branches, weeds and grass clippings are called yard wastes.

*Visitors at amusement parks throw away tons of cups, napkins, film boxes and other trash each year.*

# THE TRASH MONSTER

Trash is like a scary monster from an old movie. It's ugly and smelly, always hanging around, and hard to get rid of.

How big is our trash monster? Scientists say every person in the United States makes about three pounds of trash every day of every year. That's 810 million pounds of trash a day!

People must get rid of trash safely and carefully. Litter, junk and garbage not only make our neighborhoods look bad—they attract rats and bugs, and cause disease.

*Uncaring people dumped this trash beside the road because the landfill was closed.*

# THE TRASH TRAIL

The trash trail starts in our homes. People throw food scraps, used cans and boxes, papers and other things into wastebaskets.

They empty wastebaskets into garbage cans outside for trash pickup.

*Used tires are difficult to recycle and pollute the air when they are burned.*

*These plastic bottles were collected at a recycling center and will be remade into useful things.*

Garbage workers empty the trash into an open bin at the back of their trucks. Garbage trucks can haul five or six tons of trash. Each truck costs $130,000 or more to buy.

# WHERE DOES TRASH GO?

The garbage workers who collect trash in your community have a big job. People make so much trash, trash collectors are running out of safe places to put it.

Some garbage trucks dump their loads in **sanitary landfills**—places where it is safe to store trash. Landfills need lots of room. Already crowded cities don't have space for them. We need to find new ways to get rid of trash.

Sometimes people burn garbage in huge fireplaces called **incinerators.** When people burn trash, lots of smoke and ash can pollute, or poison, clean air.

*Special trucks haul trash from homes and businesses to landfills, incinerators and recycling centers.*

# TRASH AND TROUBLE

Trash can be harmful to the environment. Garbage and rubbish poison our soil, water and air when they are not handled safely.

Scientists say 14 billion tons of trash is dumped in the ocean every year. This trash kills thousands of whales, dolphins, fish, turtles and sea birds.

Now you can even find trash in outer space, orbiting the Earth. This space junk includes tools, cameras, and parts from rockets and satellites.

*In the past, life was simpler. People had fewer things, made less trash and loved the environment.*

# RECYCLING TRASH

Today, people **recycle** trash. Families and businesses are sorting their trash and taking it to recycling centers. People try to recycle aluminum cans, paper and cardboard, glass and plastic.

*Thousands of aluminum cans have been crushed to save space.*

*Let's "give a hoot" and pick up trash wherever we find it.*

Sometimes they pick out useful material from the half-eaten tuna sandwiches, gum wrappers and other garbage. Then recyclers wash and save what they find.

Trash is valuable. New paper, cans, bottles and plastics are made from those people recycle. Recycling saves money and helps stop pollution.

# WHAT CAN YOU DO?

Recycling and reusing helps solve the trash problem.

Caring businesses and families *sort out*—not *throw out*—their trash. People can take glass, plastic, paper and metal from the trash to recycling centers.

People can also recycle yard wastes into plant food called compost. This mix of rotting leaves, weeds and grass clippings is rich food for gardens and lawns.

*This student dresses as a recycling bin to show how caring people can help the environment.*

# ADOPT A ROADWAY

INDIAN RIVER COUNTY
FLORIDA

LITTER   CONTROL   BY

## TREASURE   COAST
## PILOT   CLUB

# GLOSSARY

**environment** (en VI ren ment) — the world around us, including plants, animals, soil, water and air

**gaseous waste** (GAS ee us WAIST) — smoke, exhaust and fumes

**incinerator** (in SIN ur ay ter) — a special fireplace for burning trash

**liquid waste** (LI kwid WAIST) — sewage from sinks and toilets

**recycle** (ree SY kul) — to save and remake useful things out of cans, paper and glass

**sanitary landfill** (SAN i tayr ee LAND fil) — a place made safe to dump trash

**solid waste** (SAH lid WAIST) — trash, garbage, refuse, debris, litter, junk

**toxic** (TAHKS ik) — harmful, poisonous

*In some places, sections of road are kept litter-free by people who care about the environment.*

# INDEX

appliances  8

batteries  8

cans  18, 19

compost  20

Earth  5, 17

environment  5, 17

garbage  6, 11, 12, 13, 17

garbage trucks  13, 14

garbage workers  13, 14

gaseous waste  7

glass  18, 20

incinerators  14

junk  11

landfills  14

liquid waste  7

litter  6, 11

needles  8

outer space  17

paint  8

plastic  18, 19, 20

recycle  18, 20

recycling centers  18, 20

rubbish  6, 17

scientists  7, 11, 17

solid waste  7

space junk  17

trash  5, 6, 8, 11, 12, 13, 17, 18, 19

white goods  8

yard waste  8, 20